# THE UNTAMED WORLD

# *Florida Manatees*

## J. D. Taylor

Chicago, Illinois

Published by Raintree, a division of Reed Elsevier, Inc.

Library of Congress Cataloging-in-Publication Data

Taylor, J. David.
 Florida manatees / J.D. Taylor.
     p. cm. -- (The Untamed world)
Summary: Describes the physical characteristics, classification,
behavior, habitat, and endangered status of Florida manatees.
Includes bibliographical references (p.     ).
 ISBN 0-7398-6844-6 (lib. bdg. : hardcover)
 1. West Indian manatee--Florida--Juvenile literature. [1. Manatees. 2.
Endangered species.] I. Title. II. Series.
 QL737.S63T4 2003
 599.55'09759--dc21

                        2003006014

Printed in the United States of America
1 2 3 4 5 6 7 8 9 0  07 06 05 04 03

**Project Editor**
Heather Kissock
**Raintree Editor**
Jim Schneider
**Design and Illustration**
Warren Clark
Martha Jones
**Copy Editor**
Tina Schwartzenberger
**Layout**
Bryan Pezzi

**Consultants**
Suzanne Tarr, Staff Biologist, Save the Manatee Club
Mark Rosenthal, Lincoln Park Zoo, Chicago, IL
**Acknowledgments**
The publisher wishes to thank Warren Rylands for inspiring this series.

**Photograph Credits**
**Corel Corporation:** pages 5, 9R; **Hulton Archive:** page 47; **Mondragon Photography/Jeff Mondragon:** cover, pages 4, 6, 11, 12, 17, 20, 22, 25, 27, 29, 30, 42, 53, 56, 60; **Save the Manatee:** pages 9T (P. Rose), 39 (P. Rose), 61 (P. Rose); **Tom Stack & Associates:** pages 43 (J. Foott), 57 (J. Foott); **J.D. Taylor:** pages 7, 9B, 10, 13, 14, 16, 18, 19, 26, 31, 33, 34, 36, 37, 40, 44, 54; **U.S. Fish and Wildlife Service:** pages 21 (J. Reid), 24 (G. Rathburn), 28 (G. Rathburn), 35, 41 (J. Reid), 45 (G. Rathburn), 59 (J. Reid).

# Contents

# Introduction

*The Florida manatee is sometimes called a sea cow because it eats sea grass and other marine plants.*

In the warm waters off the coast of Florida lives a fascinating animal called the manatee. This quiet, gentle animal has been mistaken for many other creatures, ranging from a walrus to a mermaid. It may be difficult to see the resemblance between a manatee and a mermaid, but the manatee shares visible similarities with the walrus. These similarities are surprising considering that the walrus and the manatee are not closely related. In fact, the manatee is actually a closer relative of the elephant.

In this book, you will discover the world of the Florida manatee. Learn how this animal can stay underwater. Find out why the manatee cannot drink salt water. Turn the page to enter the watery world of the Florida manatee.

*Manatees are more closely related to elephants than they are to any marine mammal.*

# Features

**Manatees are specially adapted to life in the water.**

Manatees see well. They can distinguish between objects of different sizes, colors, and patterns.

**M**anatees are **mammals**. They share the same features that all mammals, including humans, share. They are warm blooded and they breathe air. They also give birth to live young, who they nurse with milk produced in their **mammary glands**. Like all mammals, the manatee has hair, but it is scattered over its body.

Manatees are specially adapted to life in the water. They lack a defined neck, so their bodies have a blimp-like shape that helps the manatee glide smoothly through water. Also, their flat, rounded tail and two front flippers are designed for moving around their water homes. These features, along with several others, provide this large animal with an ideal body for its aquatic lifestyle.

A manatee's tail and front flippers look a little like paddles.

# Classification

The Florida manatee is a subspecies of the West Indian manatee. There are three species of manatee. They are the West Indian manatee, the Amazonian manatee, and the West African manatee. These three species belong to the order of animals called Sirenia. All Sirenians share common features, including a tube-shaped body, short flippers, a flattened tail, and an aquatic lifestyle. All Sirenians are plant-eaters.

The order Sirenia is divided into two families. Manatees belong to the family *Trichechidae*. The other family, *Dugongidae*, contains the dugongs, which are animals that closely resemble the manatee.

Every known species of animal has been given a Latin name. This allows biologists who speak different languages to understand one another. The Latin name for the Florida manatee is *Trichechus manatus latirostris*.

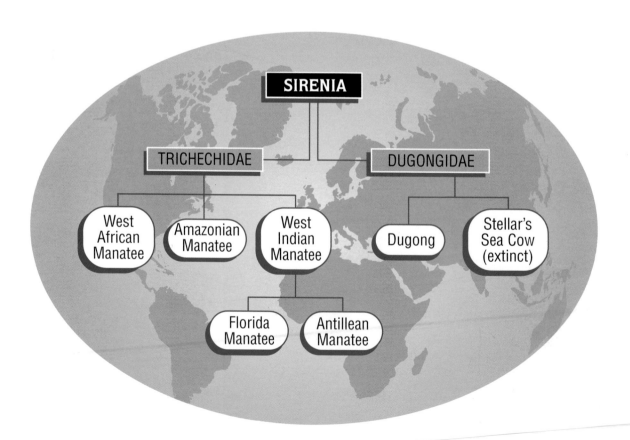

# Ancestors

Although manatees are sea mammals, they are not directly related to whales, seals, sea lions, dolphins, or walruses. The manatee's closest living relatives are the **subungulates.** An ungulate is a hoofed animal. A subungulate is an animal with poorly developed hooves. Animals belonging to the subungulate group include elephants, hyraxes, and aardvarks. These animals all share certain features with animals from the Sirenia order, including common dental characteristics and the lack of a collarbone.

Fossil evidence indicates that the first manatees appeared 13 million years ago. At this time there were several species of Sirenians living together in the warm, shallow seas that could be found all over Earth.

*The manatee's closest relatives are the elephant and a small, gopher-sized mammal called the hyrax.*

# Special Adaptations

Florida manatees have many special features that help them live in the water.

## Nostrils

As mammals, manatees need to breathe air in order to survive. This means that they must go to the water's surface when they need to breathe. Manatees breathe only through their nostrils. This allows them to feed underwater without drowning.

A manatee's nostrils are located on the top of its snout. This positioning allows the manatee to poke only its nostrils out of the water, while the rest of its body stays submerged. When the manatee has taken a breath, its nostrils close tightly with the help of valvelike flaps of skin, and the animal goes underwater again. Manatees normally take a breath every 3 to 5 minutes, but this can slow to one breath every 10 to 20 minutes when they are resting.

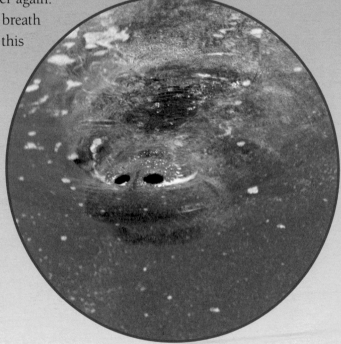

*In a single breath, a manatee can exchange 90 percent of its lung capacity.*

## Lungs

Manatees have very large lungs that lie lengthwise along their backbone. A manatee's lungs are used to store air and to control their **buoyancy**. If a manatee wants to go deep in the water, it contracts, or squeezes, its lungs. The squeezed lungs take up less space and increase the **density** of the manatee. This allows the animal to sink deeper in the water. When the manatee wants to rise to the surface, it simply expands its lung muscles, allowing the air to spread out, and floats upward.

## Bones

Manatees can remain underwater with very little effort because of their dense bones. The bones act like a diver's weight belt, which helps the diver achieve neutral buoyancy. Achieving neutral buoyancy means that the diver can stay underwater without sinking to the bottom or rising to the surface.

*The manatee is the only mammal that does not have a diaphragm. In other mammals the diaphragm is a breathing muscle located just below the lungs.*

# More Special Adaptations

## Skin

The Florida manatee's skin can be up to 2 inches (5.1 cm) thick and is rough in texture. The color of the skin ranges from brown to gray. Sometimes, the skin will have a greenish appearance. This is due to algae that often grow on the manatee's back. Much like a snake, however, a manatee sheds its skin continually. This helps get rid of the algae growth.

*Manatee skin reacts to touch because the manatee's muscles are so close to its skin. The skin contracts and slightly changes shape when scratched, bumped, or tickled.*

## Blubber

Beneath the manatee's skin is a thin layer of blubber, or fat, that is normally less than 1 inch (2.5 cm) thick. The blubber helps the manatee stay warm and survive brief periods when the temperature drops uncomfortably low.

*Manatees stay in warm waters because they have less blubber than other marine mammals. They could not survive in water that was very cold.*

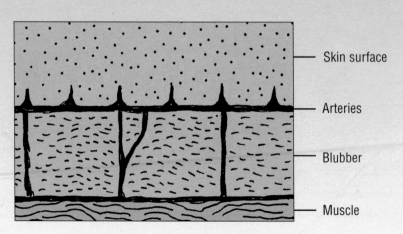

— Skin surface

— Arteries

— Blubber

— Muscle

# Tail and Flippers

A manatee uses its tail and flippers to move through water. The movement is powered by the pumping of the manatee's large, round tail. The tail moves the manatee forward and can also slow movement. All it takes is a slight angling of the tail to change the rate of movement. The flippers are used to steer the manatee in the direction it wants to go.

The flippers also maneuver the manatee along the bottom of the waterway. The manatee looks like it is walking, but it is actually using its flippers to pull itself forward. The flippers are flexible and are also used to grasp food and other items.

*A manatee's tail is large and strong. This helps the manatee travel great distances.*

# More Special Adaptations

## Mouth and Teeth

The area around a manatee's mouth is covered with short, stiff whiskers called vibrissae. The vibrissae are very sensitive to touch and are used to identify foods and nearby objects. A manatee's upper lip is **prehensile**. Divided into two sections, the upper lip is able to wrap around leaves and other plant parts so that they can be pulled into the manatee's mouth.

Behind the manatee's lips are special ridged pads that break food into smaller pieces before the molars grind it up.

Manatees eat plants that are full of **silicates** because the plants grow on the sandy bottom and are often mixed with sand. Silicates are very hard and wear out teeth. Manatees have evolved a method of feeding on silicate-rich plants that allows them to grind the food up without losing all their teeth. Manatees have "marching molars," which means that their teeth are continually replaced. New teeth emerge from the back of the manatee's jaws and slowly move forward, replacing worn teeth as the front ones fall out. A manatee has between 24 and 32 molars that are constantly being replaced over its lifetime.

# Size

The West Indian manatee is the largest of the three manatee species. When mature, Florida manatees reach an average length of between 10 feet and 12 feet (3 and 3.5 m). The largest recorded was 13 feet, 6 inches (4.1 m). Females grow to be larger than males.

An average Florida manatee weighs about 1,100 pounds (500 kg). The heaviest manatee ever recorded weighed 3,500 pounds (1,600 kg).

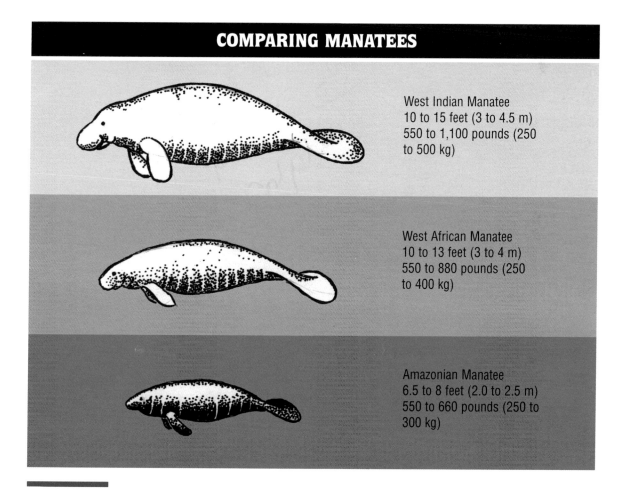

**COMPARING MANATEES**

West Indian Manatee
10 to 15 feet (3 to 4.5 m)
550 to 1,100 pounds (250 to 500 kg)

West African Manatee
10 to 13 feet (3 to 4 m)
550 to 880 pounds (250 to 400 kg)

Amazonian Manatee
6.5 to 8 feet (2.0 to 2.5 m)
550 to 660 pounds (250 to 300 kg)

*Although manatee species range in size, they all are similar in shape.*

# Social Life

**The manatee is a solitary animal.**

*Aside from whales sirenians are the only marine mammals that spend their entire lives in water.*

For the most part, the manatee is a solitary animal. When two manatees are seen together, they are usually a cow-and-calf pair. Sometimes large numbers of manatees are seen together. This group, especially if they are interacting with each other, is usually made up of a single female and several males trying to mate with her. A large number of manatees may also be seen gathering in warm water when cold weather cools the water temperature below 68 °F (20 °C).

*Although manatees may gather in groups at times, the only permanent pairings in the wild are between a mother and her calf.*

# Seasonal Activities

For the Florida manatee, the year can be divided into two seasons. During the warmer months, manatees move to favorite feeding grounds along the southern coast. They may travel as far as the Carolinas to the north and Texas to the west. It is likely that manatees follow the same routes that they traveled with their mothers.

Cold weather forces manatees to return to places where they can be reasonably assured of finding warm water. Today sources of reliable warm water are provided by power plants, which discharge heated water into Florida rivers. Manatees gather in these areas during cold weather. Counting both human-made and natural springs, there are currently 17 known major sites in Florida where manatees spend the winter.

When manatees migrate from their summer feeding areas to wintering areas, they usually follow the shoreline to avoid the deep, open ocean. They use deeper channels to get to the shallow waters where they feed and rest.

The movement of manatees away from wintering areas to summer areas allows the vegetation to replenish itself. This ensures that the manatees have a year-round supply of food.

*Manatee migration does not occur in large herds. Individuals migrate with other individuals in small groups.*

# *Mating*

When a female is ready to mate, she will attract a large number of males who compete for her attention. This mating herd may stay together for several weeks. During this time, the males shove and push each other trying to get close to the female. One male will dominate the mating for a while. When he becomes tired, he is replaced by another male, who will dominate the mating until he, too, gets tired and is replaced.

Manatees do not have a specific breeding season, and a female may be ready to mate at any time. However, mating and calving activity seems to peak in the spring and early summer.

*It is not uncommon for a female to have six to eight males in attendance. There is at least one report of a female attracting 17 males.*

# Communication

Most of the communication between manatees occurs between a mother and her calf, the basic social unit of this species. Mothers communicate with their young through high-pitched squeals. Other forms of manatee communication include body language and scent markings.

## Vocalizations

Manatees seldom make sounds with other adults. Even during mating there is little **vocalization.** Manatees do, however, send out calls to each other from time to time. Calling may signal that the manatee wants another manatee to approach, or it may indicate its own desire to approach the other manatee. These messages are conveyed through changes in pitch, loudness, duration, or harshness. Such audible communication is limited, however. When feeding or moving from one location to another, a manatee will vocalize about once every 10 minutes.

Calves and cows are most vocal when they are approaching or moving away from each other. This communication might last only a few seconds or continue for several minutes. There appear to be two reasons for this behavior. It signals that the calf is approaching to nurse or that the mother senses danger.

*Manatees do not release any air when they emit squeaking and squealing sounds.*

# Body Language

Manatees also use body language to communicate with each other. They sometimes use their bodies to push away an unwanted intruder. Usually this happens when another manatee has come too close, but they have done the same thing to divers who get too close as well. A mother will also position her body between an intruder and her calf.

# Scent Markings

Scent plays an important role in the social life of manatees. The animals leave scent markings at various sites by rubbing against objects in the vicinity. In Florida's Crystal River, where manatees have been studied closely, there are several traditional rubbing sites that are used year after year. Such rubbing sites are usually large logs or rocks. If a rubbing site, such as a sunken log, disappears, the manatees will find something else that is nearby to use. Females rub more than males do. The places on their body most often associated with rubbing are those where there are **glandular secretions**, including the area underneath their flippers and their chin.

Scientists think there are several reasons for this behavior. Rubbing may help to get rid of **parasites** that live on the manatee's skin. It may also serve to convey the female's breeding status, letting males know that she is ready to mate.

Scent marking may be referred to as a sixth sense called "smell-taste." A manatee rubs its scent on rocks or other underwater objects. Other manatees can taste these objects to help them navigate at night and locate other manatees.

# Play

*Although manatees have been known to engage in playful behavior, most of their time is spent eating, resting, and traveling.*

Manatees are intelligent and curious creatures. They demonstrate these traits through their love of play. Florida manatees take part in many fun activities and have been spotted body-surfing on fast water currents, barrel-rolling, and swimming upside down. Sometimes a group of manatees will get together to play a game of tag or follow-the-leader. Throughout these activities, the manatees can often be heard communicating with each other with various squeals and squeaks.

Manatee play even extends itself to humans. These playful creatures have been known to approach humans for a quick belly scratch or nuzzle. They have even grabbed humans with their flippers and pulled them underwater to give them a big hug.

# Wildlife Biologists Talk About Florida Manatees

## James Powell

*"Boat–manatee collisions are a problem. They are a major part of overall manatee mortality. They are also the problem that we are more likely able to do something about."*

James Powell is the Director for Aquatic Programs at the Wildlife Trust. He is an advisor to the Florida Marine Research Institute for the Florida Fish and Wildlife Conservation Commission. An international expert on manatees, his work has supported the conservation of the manatee in the Caribbean, Central America, and West Africa for more than 30 years.

## Galen Rathbun

*"It was thought that sufficient protection for manatees could be achieved by implementing local management plans. If, however, manatees are moving farther north into Georgia and the Carolinas, governmental agencies, private industry, and conservation organizations will have to reassess their strategies for protecting manatees and their habitat."*

Galen Rathbun is a marine biologist. His work with the Sirenia Project brought new insight to the plight of the Florida manatee.

## Suzanne Tarr

*"Protecting manatees protects Florida's way of life. By protecting manatees and their habitat, we ensure clean water, lush seagrass beds, and pristine habitats. We have a responsibility to make sure our grandchildren's grandchildren will get a chance to enjoy the vast array of wildlife diversity we're lucky enough to see on a regular basis."*

Suzanne Tarr is a staff biologist with the Save the Manatee Club.

# Manatee Calves

The bond between mother and calf is immediate and strong.

*A manatee calf will stay with its mother for approximately 2 years.*

Manatee mothers give birth to calves about once every 2 to 5 years. Normally only one calf is born at a time, but twins have been known to occur. The bond between mother and calf is immediate and strong as the mother takes full responsibility for raising its young. Manatee males play no role in rearing calves.

Over the next 2 to 3 years, the mother will guide the calf to adulthood. There is much for a young manatee to learn. The mother will introduce the calf to feeding areas and show the calf what it should eat. The mother will also show the calf where to find the warm waters so necessary to its survival.

*At 3 to 4 months of age, a calf begins to eat underwater vegetation, usually under the close supervision of its mother.*

# Birth

Following mating, the female often goes off on her own to seek more peaceful places to **graze** and rest. Her **gestation period** will last between 12 and 14 months. When she is ready to give birth, she will try to find a quiet area where she will not be disturbed.

The birth takes place underwater, but the calf is quickly urged to the water's surface to take its first breath of air. The calf can swim shortly after birth, but it does not stray from its mother's side. Instead, it swims closely alongside its mother so that it can nurse from the milk source located underneath its mother's flipper. Initially, the calf will nurse for 3 to 5 minutes every 1 to 2 hours, but this time increases as the calf grows and needs more milk.

*Mother manatees feed their calves and teach them what they need to know to survive on their own.*

*A manatee calf can usually swim alone within an hour of birth.*

# Care

Mothers and calves stay together for about 2 years, but the calf will only nurse for about a year. Over this 2-year period, the mother shows the calf the foods it should eat, how to migrate to warm waters, and how to play.

The mother keeps a close eye on the calf and is always on the watch for dangerous situations. If she senses danger, she will quickly take action. She may place herself between the calf and the danger, or she may sound a vocal alarm to call the calf to her side. Once the calf has come to her, both mother and calf will flee from the area.

# Development

## Birth to 2 Years

At birth, a manatee looks like a smaller version of an adult manatee, but with dark gray coloring instead of brown or light gray. The skin color becomes lighter within the manatee's first month of life. Newborns weigh about 60 pounds (27 kg) and are approximately 4 feet (1.2 m) long. Manatees can swim almost immediately after birth and begin to nurse within a few hours. By the third or fourth month of life, the calf begins to eat the underwater vegetation that its mother eats.

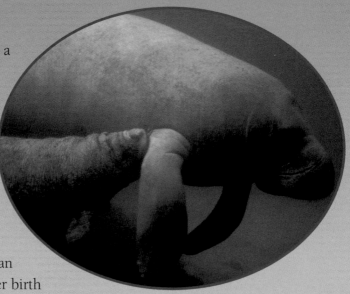

*Manatees seek out quiet areas, such as backwaters or canals, to give birth.*

The first 2 years are a time of rapid growth for the manatee. In its first year alone, its weight can jump to approximately 700 pounds (315 kg), and it can add another 2 feet (0.6 m) to its length. The calf continues to nurse throughout its first year, requiring nourishment from its mother more frequently as it continues its rapid rate of growth.

After its first year, the mother usually begins to **wean** the calf from her milk. By the end of the second year, she will have introduced the calf to the various food items available to it and to her migration routes. The calf is then ready to leave its mother's side.

## 2 to 3 Years

Not all calves leave their mothers at the 2-year mark. Those that do usually stay in nearby waters where they can maintain contact. When it is time to migrate, weaned offspring are known to tag along with their mother on the journey to their summer or winter home.

## 4 to 9 Years

By about 4 years of age, females are entering adulthood. They will be ready to mate sometime between their fourth and ninth years. A female will produce one calf every 2 to 5 years and will be able to bear young for about 20 years.

Some studies suggest that males mature later than females do, reaching adulthood when they are 6 to 9 years of age.

*As manatee calves grow older, their regular breathing rhythm will decrease from once every 20 seconds to once every 4 minutes or longer.*

Within the image, the sign reads:

MANATEE AREA
PERMITTED ACTIVITIES
PASSIVE VIEWING & SPEED
BOATING PHOTOGRAPHY
PROHIBITED ACTIVITIES
HARASSMENT LANDING DIVING
POKING HOLDING FEEDING
SWIMMING SCUBA DIVING

# Habitat

**Warm water is crucial to the survival of the manatees.**

Left: The state of Florida has established boating restriction zones to protect manatees and their habitat.

Right: Manatee sightings in Alabama, Georgia, and South Carolina waters are common during summer months.

There would be no Florida manatees if it were not for the warm-water sources along the Florida coast. In winter, most Florida manatees can be found at warm-water sources along the Florida coast. Warm water is crucial to the survival of the manatees. They will venture into more northern waters in the summer months, when the water temperature is warmer.

Unlike most other sea mammals, manatees travel in both fresh and salt water. Manatees normally stay close to shore, traveling, resting, playing, feeding, and mating in shallow water that is only 3 to 10 feet (1 to 3 m) deep.

FLORIDA MANATEES

# *Range*

Florida manatees are found in the shallow waters along the southeastern coast of the United States. They also enter rivers and lagoons. In winter most manatees are found in Florida waters, but in summer they may migrate as far north as North Carolina and as far west as Texas.

Their range is defined by water temperature. Manatees cannot tolerate water below 46 °F (8 °C) because they cannot maintain their body temperature in cold water. A manatee in water this cold will not survive long. They prefer waters with temperatures above 68 °F (20 °C). Hot summer weather allows them to expand their range as the waters along the coastline warm. The return of cold weather in fall forces the animals to retreat to areas where water is consistently warm.

A manatee can travel an average of 40 to 50 miles (64 to 80 km) a day. Some manatees, particularly males, will travel even farther. One wandering male had to be rescued from the chilly waters of Chesapeake Bay and flown back to Florida.

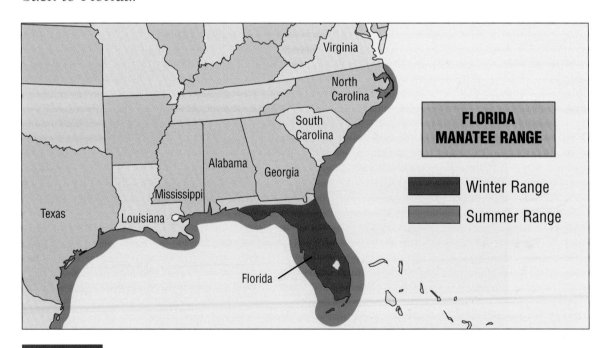

*Manatees travel more in the summer months. In the winter, they stay in the Florida area, relying on the warm, freshwater springs that are found inland.*

32

# Water Sources

Water is the key element in the Florida manatee's habitat. Although manatees can travel in both fresh and salt water, the water must be warm or the manatees will not survive. Florida is an ideal place for manatees because it has an abundance of natural springs. The average temperature of these springs ranges from 70 °F to 84 °F (21 °C to 29 °C), temperatures warm enough to support the manatee. The Crystal River spring feeds an important winter sanctuary for manatees.

*Manatees will seek quiet areas in canals, creeks, rivers, and lagoons to rest in. These areas are also used for feeding, mating, playing, and calving.*

As important as these springs are, the manatees will also use human-made sources of warm water. Electricity-generating and industrial plants along several of Florida's rivers use the water to cool down their generators. The water is cold when it comes into the plant, but it is warm when it is discharged back into the river. These plants have provided manatees with another set of warm water refuges.

Warm water is only one of the species' habitat needs. They also need abundant aquatic vegetation. They must also have access to fresh water. Like humans manatees cannot drink salt water. Their bodies are poorly equipped to get rid of excess salt, and they must drink fresh water from time to time. The perfect mixture of saltwater and freshwater habitats can be found in bays, lagoons, and estuaries that are fed with a constant source of fresh water from a river or stream.

# Food

**Manatees prefer food that does not grow too deep in the water.**

*The Florida manatee feeds on more than 60 varieties of grasses and plants, including the water lily.*

Sirenians are unique mammals. They are the only mammals in the world to feed almost exclusively on marine and freshwater vegetation. They are **herbivores** and eat a wide variety of aquatic and semiaquatic plants. They will sometimes also feed on land plants that hang over the water.

Manatees eat plant matter but may ingest other animals, such as sea squirts and mollusks, that cling to the grass they are eating. Their preferred plants include sea grass, water hyacinth, and hydrilla, all of which flourish in warm subtropical waters.

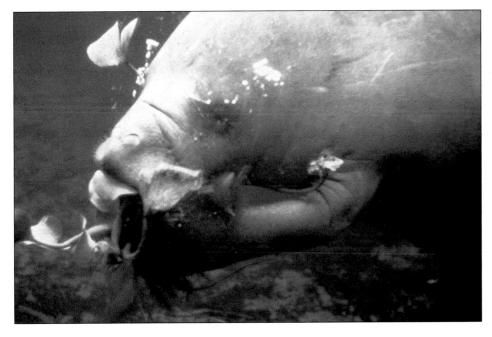

*Manatees graze for food along water floors and surfaces.*

# What They Eat

Manatees are known to eat a total of 44 different species of plants and 10 species of algae. Some of the plants that manatees eat include water hyacinth, water hydrilla, various sea grasses, and mangrove leaves. Algae are not a favorite food and are rarely eaten. Manatees avoid eating plants that have naturally occurring **toxins,** such as spatterdock and waterpennyworth. On rare occasions, manatees will swim up to a beach to eat plants along the shoreline. They have even been seen eating acorns that have fallen into the water.

Estimates of food consumption range from 8 to 20 percent of their body **mass.** The minimum amount of plant material a manatee must eat is between 4 to 8 percent of its body mass. That means, for example, that an 800-pound (360-kg) manatee would have to eat up to 32 pounds (14.5 kg) of vegetation a day. This may seem to be a large amount of food, but water plants can replace lost material much faster than land plants.

*Manatees are the main consumers of water hyacinth.*

# How They Eat

Many of the foods a manatee eats are low in nutritional value. Manatees must spend 5 to 8 hours a day feeding to get the energy and nutrients they need to survive. When they find something to eat, they wrap their prehensile lip around the food and work it into their mouths. Sometimes they grasp the food with their flippers to hold it as they graze.

To digest food that is so low in nutritional value, manatees have evolved an extra large stomach and very long intestines. The increased size of their digestive system allows them to extract the most nutrients available from their food.

*The location of the manatee's mouth is well adapted for eating bottom vegetation.*

A manatee's intestines are 150 feet (45 m) long. Between the large and small intestine is an area known as the "mid-gut cecum." This area is where much of the **cellulose** is broken down by bacteria. Manatees have one of the highest-rated abilities to break down cellulose of any living mammal.

The large body of the manatee also aids in the digestion of food. Much of the digested food energy is stored in the blubber that lies beneath the manatee's skin and around its intestines. This stored food energy helps protect the digestive process from the effects of cooler water that would slow down the process. The energy stored as blubber helps the manatee survive during long periods of fasting, especially in winter when there is not as much new plant growth.

# The Food Cycle

A food cycle shows how energy in the form of food is passed from one living thing to another. Florida manatees are herbivores, which means that they eat only plants. As they feed and move through the water, manatees affect the lives of other living things.

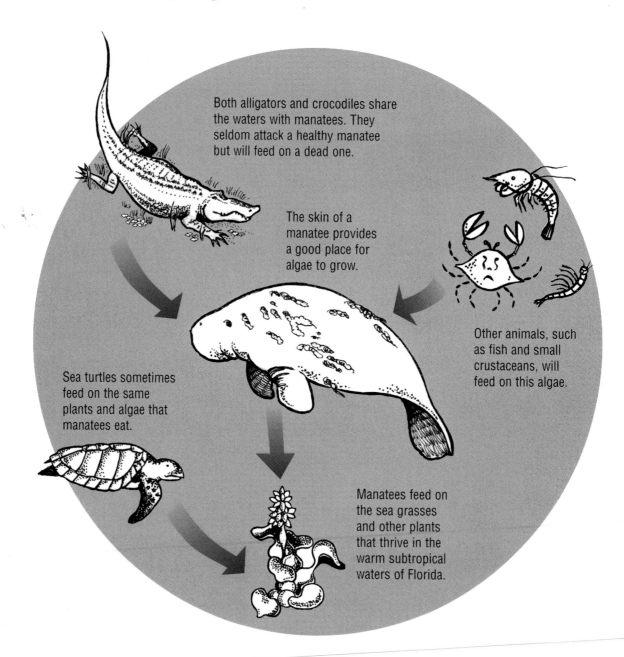

Both alligators and crocodiles share the waters with manatees. They seldom attack a healthy manatee but will feed on a dead one.

The skin of a manatee provides a good place for algae to grow.

Other animals, such as fish and small crustaceans, will feed on this algae.

Sea turtles sometimes feed on the same plants and algae that manatees eat.

Manatees feed on the sea grasses and other plants that thrive in the warm subtropical waters of Florida.

# A Florida Manatee Quiz

Try this quiz to see how much you know about
Florida manatees. Are the following statements true or false?
The answers are at the bottom of the page.

**1** A manatee has teeth that are continually replacing themselves.

**2** The West Indian manatee is the smallest of the three species of manatee.

**3** When migrating, manatees swim along the shoreline.

**4** Female adult manatees give birth once a year.

**5** Manatees are saltwater animals.

**6** Manatees are herbivores. They eat only plants.

**1) True.** As the teeth wear down, they move forward in the mouth until they fall out. At the same time, new teeth are growing in the back of the mouth.

**2) False.** The West Indian manatee is the largest species of manatee.

**3) True.** Manatees avoid the open ocean whenever possible. They travel in deep water only to access the shallow waters where they feed and rest.

**4) False.** Female adult manatees give birth once every 2 to 5 years.

**5) False.** Manatees travel in both fresh water and salt water.

**6) True.** Their diet consists of a variety of aquatic and semiaquatic plants.

# Competition

**Boating collisions lead to many manatee deaths each year.**

*Most manatees do not seek interaction with people. Female manatees are especially careful not to let humans get too close to their calves.*

Manatees have no real **predators** and live peacefully with other marine animals. While manatees can die from environmental conditions, such as cold weather, humans are by far their greatest competition. This competition comes in the form of both human activity and human progress. Boating collisions lead to many manatee deaths each year. The animals also fall victim to the development of waterway systems. Florida is a popular tourist destination. As more and more people arrive to visit and to live, changes to the environment are unavoidable. Sadly, these changes sometimes have a negative effect on the manatee and its habitat.

*Despite slow-speed and idle-speed zones posted in areas where manatees tend to congregate, many manatees suffer injuries or are killed in collisions with boats.*

41

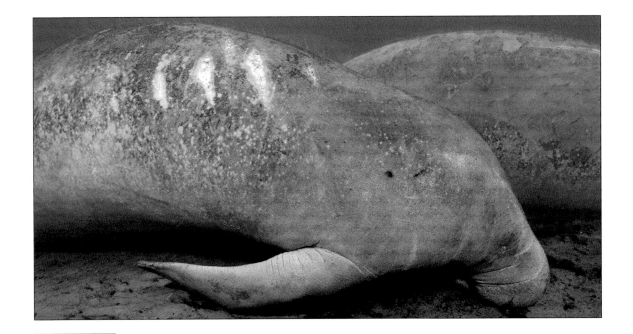

*Manatees with propeller scars are a common sight in the waters of Florida.*

# Competing with Humans

Historically manatees were hunted for their blubber and their meat. Today their single greatest threat is from motorboats. Collisions with motorboats account for approximately 25 percent of all manatee deaths in Florida. In 2002 that number increased to 33 percent when a record 95 manatees died from boat-inflicted injuries. Boating accidents are responsible for eight out of every ten human-caused manatee deaths.

In many states manatees face habitat loss as more development and an increased human population alter their habitat and drive them away from their food sources. Rivers and streams are now controlled by many man-made constructions, including floodgates and sewage systems. Manatees sometimes get caught in these systems and can be crushed or drowned as a result. The opening and closing of floodgates has been known to separate a calf from its mother, resulting in almost certain death for the calf. As the human population increases, water pollution and landfill projects are also increasing. These, too, contribute to the loss of habitat and food for the manatee.

# Red Tide

Manatees sometimes face competition from their environment. An occurrence called red tide can be devastating to manatee populations. A red tide is caused by the bloom of natural algae that stains the water a reddish-brown color. The algae carry a toxin that attacks the nervous system of any animals that come into contact with it. The animals die because they cannot breathe. In 1996 approximately 149 manatees died from a red tide in Florida that lasted the first 5 months of the year. Considering that this loss made up more than 10 percent of Florida's manatee population, the impact on this **endangered** species was enormous.

*Red tide causes paralysis in manatees. They are unable to surface and breathe, so they hold their breath until they suffocate.*

# Relationships with Other Animals

Florida manatees share the water with many other sea creatures, including various fish and turtle species, river otters, alligators, and crocodiles. Manatees are not aggressive and tend to avoid confrontations with their neighbors. If threatened by another animal, they will flee instead of standing their ground. Their submissive nature leads to a peaceful coexistence with the other animals in their waters.

Even the alligator tends to leave the manatee alone, probably because of its massive size. The manatee's large size, its tough hide, and its preference for near-shore waters help it avoid any other predators large enough to be a threat.

*Scientists are uncertain what danger, if any, other sea creatures in its habitat pose for the manatee.*

# Relationships with Other Manatees

Except for the mother and calf unit, manatees are mostly solitary animals. Solitary species tend to have fewer interactions with other members of their species, and therefore have less need to develop complex social systems. This is not to say, however, that manatees avoid contact with one another. Groups of manatees come together for mating, and adolescent manatees have been known to join their mothers during migration. Sometimes, manatees encounter other manatees in a random fashion by merely swimming in the same waters.

*Manatees usually form groups to find food or mates or to avoid predators. Whales, dolphins, seals, and sea otters behave in a similar way.*

Scientists have observed some of these encounters and have noted specific behaviors showing that, as solitary as these animals can be at times, they do enjoy being with other manatees. Manatees have been observed swimming together, diving together, and even body-surfing with each other. They even appear to recognize each other at times. When two manatees meet, they often greet one another with a "kiss," nuzzling their mouths against each other's body. Scientists have also observed manatees hugging each other with their flippers and sharing a nap on the water's floor with their tails touching.

# Folklore

In 1493 Christopher Columbus explored the area now known as the Caribbean. His crew became excited when they sighted what they thought were mermaids. They saw lovely creatures rise out of the water and return to their underwater world with a quick splash of their tails. From far away, they probably looked like they were half-woman, half-fish, but most people now believe these men saw manatees.

The idea of manatees as seamaidens continued over time and contributed to the naming of the Sirenian order. The root word of "Sirenian" is "siren." In ancient Greek mythology, sirens were sea nymphs that lured sailors with their beauty and their songs. When the sailors tried to get closer to the nymphs, their boats would crash against the rocks.

*Christopher Columbus wrote in his log that the mermaids he saw were not as beautiful as sailors' stories suggested they would be.*

# Folklore History

Manatees share a long history with the native groups of the Caribbean. In most cases, the manatee was a food source for these people. As a result, their folklore centers around hunting and food preparation rituals.

The Rama people of Nicaragua believed that the manatee was an intelligent animal that had extremely good hearing. When hunting, the Rama would not talk about where they thought they should hunt or how they would capture the manatee. They were afraid that the animal would hear them and leave the area.

After a successful hunt, the person who caught the manatee was given its earbones. The Rama believed that manatees could not hear a person who wore another manatee's earbones. Manatee earbones were also used as charms to ward off witchcraft in the Yucatan, and to ease the pain of childbirth in Guatemala.

*The Rama believed that it was important to be quiet when hunting the manatee.*

# Myths vs. Facts

**Manatees are slow-moving creatures.**

Manatees normally travel between 3 and 5 miles (4.8 and 8.0 km) per hour. However, they can move faster if necessary, traveling up to 20 miles (32.2 km) per hour in short bursts.

**Manatees are clumsy.**

Manatees are designed for underwater life. Their shape helps them move gracefully through the water. They can often be observed performing somersaults and other acrobatic activities.

**Manatees were brought to Florida in the mid-1900s to control the growth of water hyacinth.**

Fossil remains indicate that manatees have lived in the Florida area for about 45 million years. Water hyacinth is a nuisance plant in Florida, but manatees contribute little to growth control. While manatees do eat water hyacinth, they are not able to eat it as quickly as it grows.

# Folktales

Throughout history, the manatee's mystical presence has generated many stories. Early native groups believed that they shared common bonds with the manatee. Sailors brought stories about mermaids home to Europe, where they inspired a classic fairy tale. The manatee continues to intrigue and amaze people all over the world.

## Creation Stories

The Warauno, a South American people, believe that the manatee has human beginnings. Warauno legend tells the story of two sisters who are always fighting. One sister moves away to the forest with her son, but the other sister follows and puts a curse on both her sister and the son, turning them into hoofed animals called tapirs. The other sister is cursed in return. She and her unborn child are forced to live their lives in the water, where they become the first manatees.

In Brazil, some native groups also believe that the manatee has a human beginning. They believe that there is an underwater city at the bottom of the Orinoco River. Any human who travels to the city and eats the food is transformed into a manatee.

## The Little Mermaid

The manatee–human connection was further strengthened when Hans Christian Andersen developed the story of "The Little Mermaid" in 1836. In this well-known fairy tale, a young mermaid falls in love with a human prince. She gives up her voice in exchange for legs so that she can be with the prince. The pair go through many experiences before they live happily ever after.

## Chessie the Traveler

A modern folktale is currently evolving along the Atlantic coast of the United States. In 1994 a male manatee was sighted in Chesapeake Bay, hundreds of miles north of the typical manatee's range. The manatee was given the name Chessie, and he was a big celebrity until the weather turned cold. Fearing for his health, scientists captured the manatee and flew him back to the warmer waters of Florida. The next year, Chessie did it all again, making the 500-mile (800-km) journey back to Chesapeake Bay. In fact, he went further, this time going as far north as Rhode Island before turning back to Florida.

The legend of Chessie continues into the 21st century. In August 2001 Chessie was spotted in the waters off Virginia. Chessie is now the subject of a book published by the Humane Society. To find out more about this traveling manatee, read: *Chessie, the Travelin' Man* by Randy Houk (Humane Society of the United States, 1997).

# Protecting Manatees in Florida

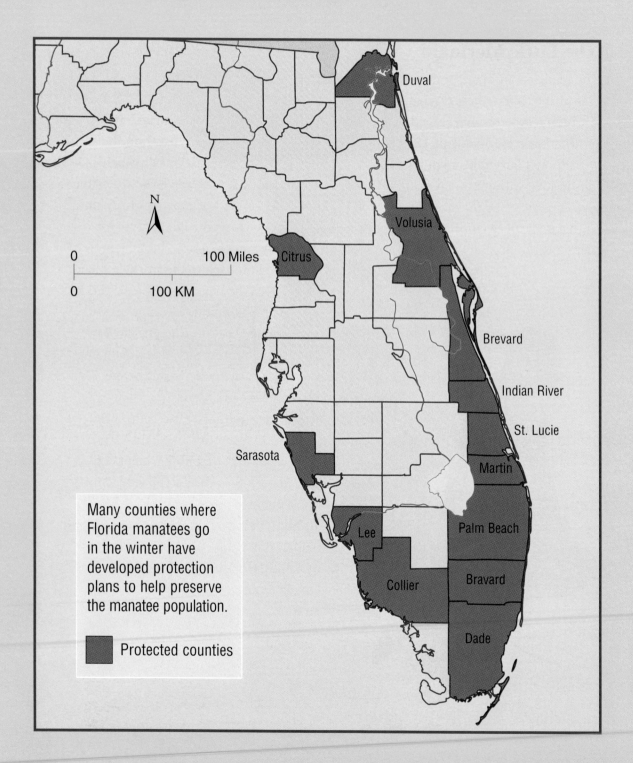

Duval

Volusia

Citrus

Brevard

Indian River

St. Lucie

Sarasota

Martin

Lee

Palm Beach

Collier

Bravard

Dade

Many counties where Florida manatees go in the winter have developed protection plans to help preserve the manatee population.

Protected counties

0                    100 Miles

0                    100 KM

N

# *Status*

**The U.S. Marine Mammal Protection Act has protected manatees in Florida waters since 1972.**

In 2001 the Florida manatee population was estimated at close to 3,200. In some small areas, scientists believe that the numbers have increased since the animal was given protection under the law. Many are concerned, however, that this growth may not continue. In some larger areas where deaths are alarmingly high, scientists believe the population is declining. The U.S. Marine Mammal Protection Act has protected manatees in Florida waters since 1972. This act banned the hunting, harassment, and killing of manatees and forbade trade in manatee parts. Manatees are also protected under the U.S. Endangered Species Act of 1973. Under this act the manatee was declared an endangered species.

The manatee received further legal status in 1978 under the Florida Marine Sanctuary Act. This act allowed Florida to establish sanctuaries for manatees where boating is off limits.

*The state of Florida adopted new standards for listing endangered and threatened species in 1999. Florida manatees may be reclassified as only threatened, although there has been no significant increase in population.*

# Protecting the Manatee

To help put an end to tragic deaths of the Florida manatee, the U.S. Fish and Wildlife Service has developed a manatee recovery plan. As a result boat regulations are in place around the areas where manatees are common. "Go slow" warnings have been posted on rivers frequented by manatees, and in some areas, boats are banned from key areas. The service has also developed sanctuaries where manatees are able to live

*Idle speed, the lowest speed required to maintain steering, and slow zones are two ways that Florida is trying to protect manatees.*

in relative peace. Fines are imposed on those who threaten or harm manatees, and construction companies operating in waters where manatees are known to travel must post signs warning workers that manatees are found there. If a manatee enters the area, it may be necessary to halt work until it leaves. Scientists are constantly reviewing the situation with an eye toward helping the manatee.

The manatee has benefited from this process. Data provided by researchers shows slight population growth in recent years in small areas where manatees have been well protected for a long time. Local citizens and tourists have helped by reporting injured or dead manatees. This has helped biologists link human activities to manatee deaths.

Many problems remain. Manatees are still killed in boat collisions, they still die entangled in fishing nets, they still ingest fishing lures, and they still get crushed and drowned in locks and flood-control structures. A growing human population is putting more and more demands on Florida's water resources, threatening natural springs. Aging power plants, so important for the warm water they provide, may have to be rebuilt. This may deprive manatees of the warm waters they need in the winter.

# Viewpoints

## Should Florida manatees remain a protected species?

Politicians, scientists, and boating enthusiasts constantly debate the protected status of the Florida manatee. Some people feel that there are now enough manatees swimming in Florida waters and that the protected status designation should be removed. Others feel that the manatee population is still too fragile to be maintained without protection.

### PRO

**1** Protecting the Florida manatee is the only way to maintain the wild population and promote its growth.

**2** Manatees have a slow reproduction rate. Protecting the manatee ensures that the population has time to grow.

**3** Manatees are not aggressive animals and have little means of defense. Giving them protected status helps keep people from harassing, injuring, and killing the animals.

### CON

**1** Large numbers of manatees would threaten the existence of other threatened and endangered species, including sea grass.

**2** Manatee populations are becoming a nuisance in some areas, especially around power plants, where they are now occurring in high numbers. A population boom affects the entire **ecosystem** by destroying plants native to the area and by reducing the food available to other wildlife.

**3** Protecting the manatee and allowing the population to grow may eventually prevent Florida from developing its tourism and real estate projects, thus affecting the economy.

# The Sirenia Project

The Sirenia Project, based in Gainesville, Florida, was established more than 25 years ago to study and monitor the life of the Florida manatee. It is staffed by a group of scientists dedicated to helping the manatee survive in the modern world.

The scientists in the Sirenia Project have photographed and cataloged manatees, paying close attention to the scars that mark them. Researchers developed an image-based computer program to identify permanently marked manatees. Most manatees have had encounters with boat propellers. The scar patterns from these run-ins are as individual as human fingerprints.

The information helps scientists track specific manatees and create a history of their lives. Each time a scientist identifies a manatee, information on its location, its activities, and its possible companions is added to the database. Over time this information creates a profile of individual manatees. This information helps scientists learn more about individual manatees and about manatees in general. As of 1999 more than 1,400 manatees, representing nearly half all of the manatees living in Florida waters, had been entered in the database.

*Propeller scars create unique patterns on a manatee's body. Scientists use these patterns to identify and track individual manatees.*

*Tracking devices have enabled scientists to document long-distance movements of individual manatees. This information helps establish appropriate protection for their vulnerable habitats.*

# Tracking the Florida Manatee

Following manatees has become easier with advanced radio and satellite tracking devices. It is no longer necessary to actually see the manatee to know where it is located.

When tracking a manatee, scientists attach a small portable tracking unit to a belt attached to the manatee's body. The unit sends out a series of beeps in a particular pattern that allows the scientist to identify the manatee. If tracking by radio, the scientist follows the signal from a boat or plane. Satellite tracking uses a similar system, but its receivers are mounted on satellites circling Earth. These satellites pass over Florida nine times every 24 hours. On each pass, the location of the manatee is downloaded into a computer. The scientist may be hundreds of miles from the manatee.

These two systems make it possible to track the movements of manatees 24 hours a day, something that would be very difficult for field researchers to do if they had to watch the manatee from the ground. These systems allow the researchers to identify key areas of manatee habitat and make suitable recommendations to protect them.

# What You Can Do

Florida manatees are fascinating animals that need our help. You can learn more about them by writing to a conservation group or government organization for more information.

## Conservation Groups

**Sirenia Project (Manatee Research)**
412 NE 16th Avenue, Room 250
Gainesville, Florida
32601-3701

**Save the Manatee Club**
500 N. Maitland Avenue
Maitland, Florida
32751

**Wildlife Trust**
1600 Ken Thompson Parkway
Sarasota, Florida
34236

**Harbor Branch Oceanographic**
5600 US 1 North
Fort Pierce, Florida
34946

## Government

**Florida Fish and Wildlife Conservation Commission**
620 South Meridian Street
Tallahassee, Florida
32399-1600

**Florida Marine Research Insitute**
100 Eighth Avenue SE
St. Petersburg, Florida
33701-5095

**Homosassa Springs State Wildlife Park**
4150 S. Suncoast Boulevard
Homosassa, Florida
34446

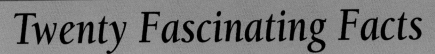

# Twenty Fascinating Facts

**1** Manatees can tell one color from another.

**2** Florida manatees were not the first members of the Sirenia class to live in Florida waters. For a long time, the tropical waters of the Western Hemisphere were home to at least three now-extinct species of dugong.

**3** The first true manatees were found in Florida waters 2 to 3 million years ago. They evolved in the waters of the Amazon and other South American rivers and spread north. It was during this period that they developed renewable teeth that could withstand the wear and tear of eating silicates.

**4** The Florida manatee population can be divided into four sub-populations. The largest population, consisting of 46 percent, is found on the Atlantic coast. The Upper St. Johns River has about 4 percent of the population. Southwestern Florida has the second largest population with 38 percent. Northwest Florida has 12 percent of the population.

**5** An extreme cold snap in the winter of 1989–1990 killed more than 50 manatees in Florida waters.

**6** The manatee is known by different names around the world. The Portuguese call it *peixe-boi*, or fish cow, and the Spanish call it *vaca marina*, or sea cow.

**7** The ratio of males to females is 1:1. This means that there are equal numbers of males and females in the manatee population.

**8** Tampa Bay is home to 350 manatees in the winter months and approximately 150 in the summer.

**9** Manatees are capable of exchanging 90 percent of their lung capacity in one breath. Humans can exchange only 10 to 15 percent of their stale air for fresh air.

**10** Manatees are remarkably resistant to natural diseases. They have a very efficient and responsive immune system.

**11** Manatees rest from 2 to 12 hours a day, depending on the season. They remain motionless, either on the surface or on the bottom of the sea floor.

**12** The manatee's thick skin is a bit jiggly under its neck and flippers.

**13** The algae that grow on the manatee's skin are home to small animals, including small crustaceans and mollusks.

**14** Florida's native peoples used to call manatees "big beavers" because of their large, flat tails.

**15** The Amazonian manatee is the only manatee that lives its entire life in fresh water.

**16** So many manatees have propeller scars that scientists use the marks to identify manatees.

**17** Manatee eyelids are transparent and slide across the eye instead of down. Manatees do not have eyelashes.

**18** Most mammals have seven neck vertebrae. The manatee has only six. This means that the manatee cannot turn its head when it wants to see what is behind it. Instead, the manatee must turn its entire body around.

**19** It is illegal to feed, touch, or provide fresh water to a manatee. All of these actions may encourage the manatee to approach people and place it in harm's way.

**20** Once a manatee has died, its inner earbones are used to estimate the animal's age. Scientists count growth layers in the same way they would count the rings in a tree.

# Glossary

**buoyancy:** Ability to float in fluid

**cellulose:** Tough material that forms the walls of plant cells

**density:** Thickness

**ecosystem:** All the living and nonliving things in a certain area

**endangered:** Species of animal that is close to becoming extinct

**gestation period:** The time a female is pregnant

**glandular secretions:** Substance that oozes from a body organ

**graze:** To feed on grasses and plants

**herbivores:** Animals that feed solely on plants

**mammals:** Animals that are warm-blooded and have a backbone

**mammary glands:** Body parts that produce milk

**mass:** Size or bulk

**parasites:** Animals or plants that live on another animal or plant

**predators:** Animals that live by hunting other animals for food

**prehensile:** Specially adapted for gripping objects

**silicates:** Any of the largest group of minerals

**subungulates:** Animals with poorly developed hooves

**toxins:** Poisons

**vocalization:** Sound made to send messages to others or to express emotions

**wean:** To gradually remove a young animal from its mother's milk

# Suggested Reading

Feeney, Kathy. *Manatees*. Minnetonka, Minn.: NorthWord Press, 2001.

Ripple, Jeff. *Manatees and Dugongs of the World*. Stillwater, Minn.: Voyageur Press, Inc., 1999.

Sleeper, Barbara. *In the Company of Manatees*. New York: Three Rivers Press, 2000.

Walker, Sally M. *Manatees*. Minneapolis, Minn.: Carolrhoda Books, Inc., 1999.

## FLORIDA MANATEES ON THE INTERNET

One of the places you can find out more about Florida manatees is on the Internet. Visit the following sites, or try searching one of your own:

### Sea World

http://www.seaworld.org/animalbytes/manateeab.html

### Manatee: The Web Site for Manatee Watchers

http://www.homesafe.com/manatee

### U.S. Geological Survey: Center for Aquatic Resources Studies

http://www.fcsc.usgs.gov/Manatees/manatees.html

# Index